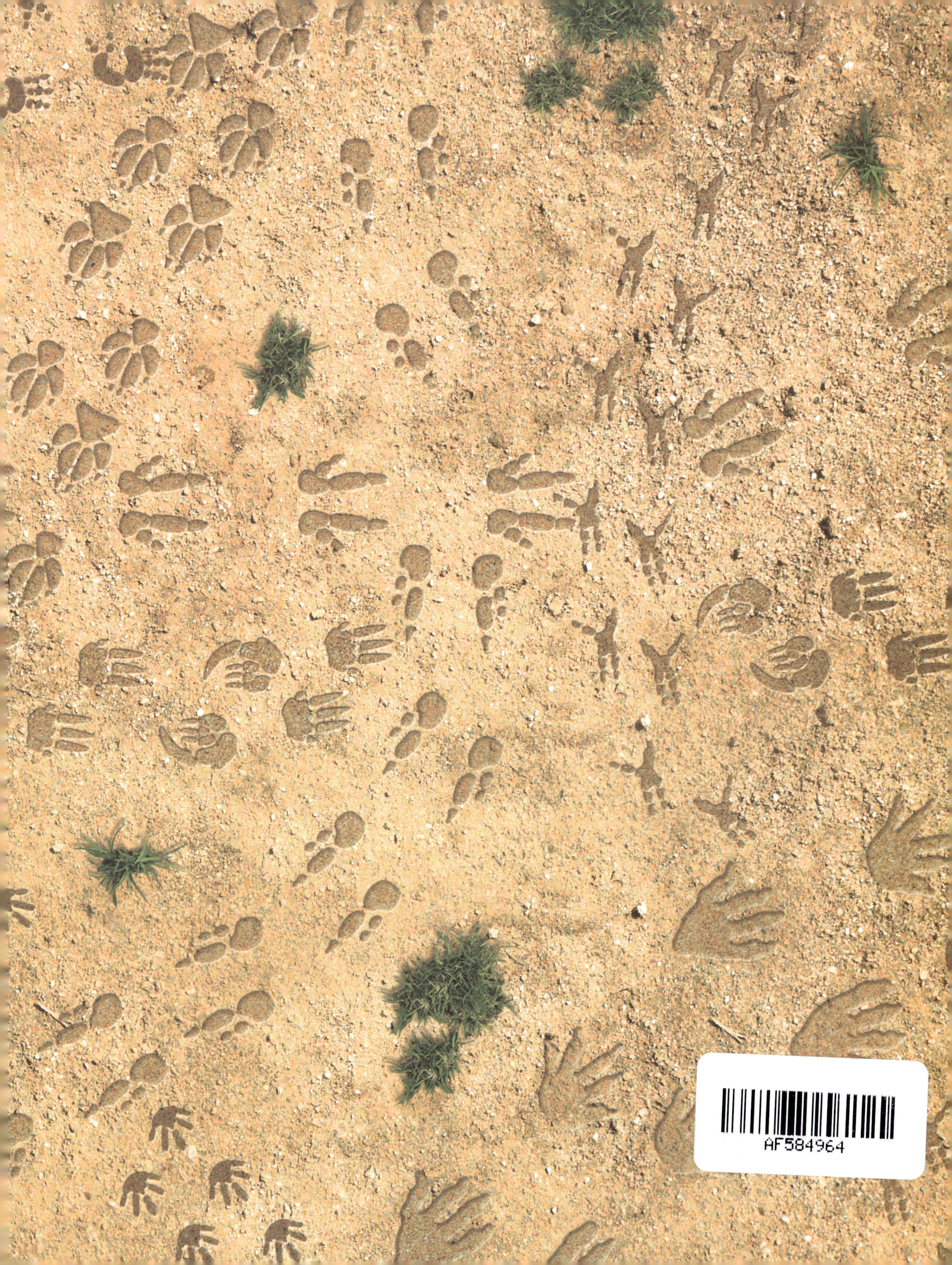

AUSTRALIA'S REMARKABLE WILDLIFE

JOHN LESLEY

CROCODILE

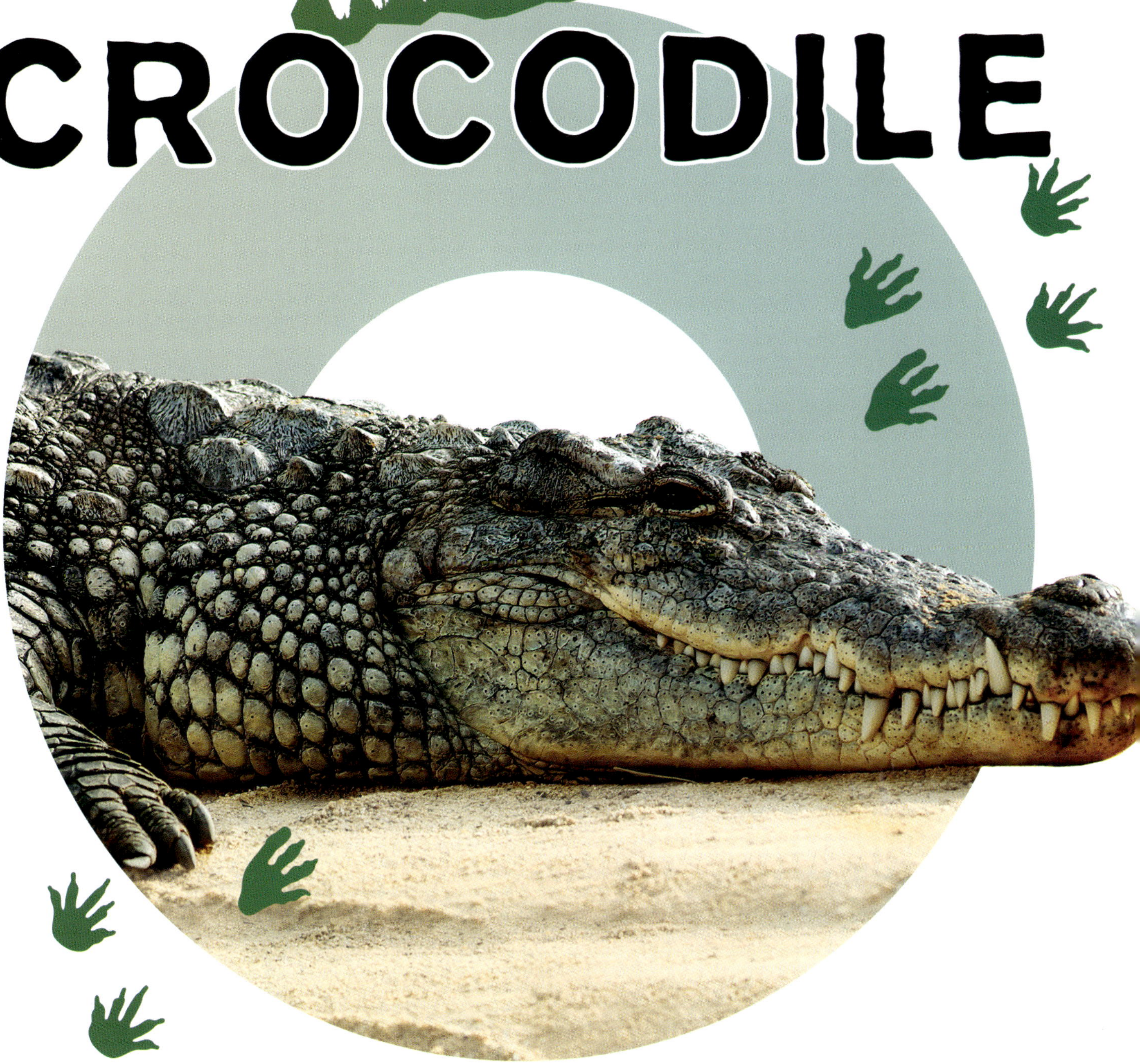

First Published 2022 by
Redback Publishing
PO Box 357 Frenchs Forest NSW 2086
Australia

www.redbackpublishing.com
orders@redbackpublishing.com

ISBN 978-1-925860-95-5

Author: John Lesley
Editor: Caroline Thomas
Design: Redback Publishing

NATIONAL LIBRARY OF AUSTRALIA

A catalogue record for this book is available from the National Library of Australia

Originated by Redback Publishing

Printed and bound in Malaysia

Acknowledgements
Abbreviations: l—left, r—right, b—bottom, t—top, c—centre, m—middle
We would like to thank the following for permission to reproduce photographs: (Images © shutterstock) p13br Mark Marathon via Wikimedia Commons, p18cm and p32 Tom Jastram.

CONTENTS

CROCODILE BASIC FACTS

SCIENTIFIC NAME

There are two types of crocodiles in Australia:

Crocodylus porosus - the saltwater crocodile

Crocodylus johnstoni - the freshwater crocodile

TYPE OF ANIMAL

Reptile

SIZE

Males can grow to about six metres long. The adult Australian saltwater crocodile is the largest reptile in the world.

Saltwater crocodiles

COLOUR

Brown, black or grey mottled skin

CONSERVATION STATUS

In the mid 1900s, hunters reduced the number of crocodiles to very low levels. Since they were on a pathway to extinction, crocodiles were protected by law in the 1970s. Numbers have now increased and Australian crocodiles no longer face extinction.

Saltwater crocodile

SALTIES AND FRESHIES

Saltwater crocodiles, or salties, swim in the ocean near beaches and at the mouths of rivers. They also travel upstream into freshwater.

Freshwater crocodiles, or freshies, live in rivers, lakes and billabongs. They walk across land to find food or a better waterway to live in. Freshies are a little smaller than salties, but people often cannot tell the difference when they see one. In the dry season, freshies hide in shelters they dig into the sides of waterways.

THE CROCODILE BODY

Eyes on top of the head - allows them to see prey on the surface or on land while still hiding underwater.

Nose - the nostrils are on the top of the snout, allowing the crocodile to stay hidden underwater.

Bony plates in the thick skin - protects them from attack by other animals.

Long, thick tail - used to help them swim and as a weapon.

Mottled skin colour - helps them hide in shallow water or in the shade under trees and bushes on land.

ARE CROCODILES REALLY DANGEROUS?

YES! CROCODILES HAVE KILLED PEOPLE AND PETS.

In the Northern Territory in Australia, the government has a BE CROCWISE program. Its role is to advise people on safety measures to take to avoid being attacked by a crocodile. Any waterway in the Top End could have crocodiles lurking in it.

There are about the same number of people in the Top End as there are crocodiles.

HOW FAST ARE THEY?

Crocodiles will stay still underwater, waiting for an animal to come near. They will then strike very quickly. Although they have short legs, crocs can move very quickly on land, reaching speeds of around 14 kilometres per hour over a short distance. In comparison, a person can jog at about 6-9 kilometres per hour.

Crocodiles will often strike from below water

Crocodiles can move very quickly on land

CROCODILE TEETH

One of the features that separate crocodiles from alligators is that some of the crocodile's teeth can protrude from the sides of its closed mouth.

Crocodiles have a very strong downward bite, but a much weaker upward strength in their jaws.

This allows hunters to restrain them by tying their jaws together. The crocodile's lower jaw is too weak to snap the rope.

Crocodile teeth have evolved to hold prey underwater to drown. The teeth then break the dead animal into big chunks before the crocodile swallows its meal.

A crocodile has the strongest bite of any animal.

CROCODILE HABITATS

Crocodiles live in the northern parts of Western Australia, Queensland and the Northern Territory, as well as on islands in the northern regions. They can swim long distances across the ocean to reach these islands.

Crocodiles live in both saltwater and freshwater. Some can even survive the dry season by hiding in burrows. Beaches, lakes, billabongs, mangrove swamps and rivers are all possible habitats for crocodiles in Australia's Top End.

CROCODILE LIFE CYCLE

Crocodile nest

EGGS

Crocodiles lay eggs in warm sand or soil near a waterway. The female crocodile usually stays nearby, often lying hidden underwater to check that the nest is not disturbed. The eggs hatch after about 90 days. Once the eggs hatch, the female crocodile gently scoops the babies up in her mouth, and takes them to a spot where they can start to hunt for themselves.

LIFE SPAN

Crocodiles can live for 70 years.

CROCODILE ANCESTORS

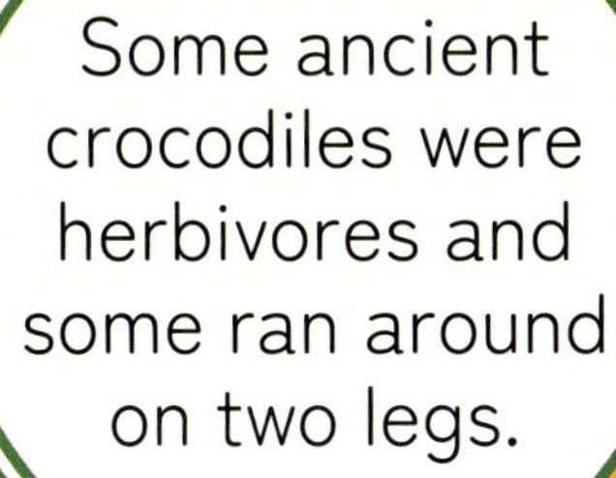

Some ancient crocodiles were herbivores and some ran around on two legs.

Crocodiles have been around for about 200 million years, during which time some of them reached lengths of up to 40 metres. Crocodiles are not modern dinosaurs, even though they look like them.

Quinkana was a 7 metre long Australian crocodile that only died out about 40,000 years ago. This was well within the time period when ancestors of the Indigenous people were living in Australia. Qunikana had longer legs than a modern crocodile, which would have allowed it to run much faster. What a terrifying thought!

HUNTER AND HUNTED

WHAT DO CROCODILES EAT?

Crocodiles are carnivores. They will eat birds, frogs, mammals, fish and any other meat source they can catch. They grab their prey with their strong teeth and jaws, then pull it underwater and drown it.

Crocs will eat a dead animal if they find one. In some cases, crocodiles even eat each other. If there is leftover meat, a croc will hide it underwater for later.

To help them digest their food, crocodiles eat small stones, which help to grind the food up inside their gizzard. Birds also have gizzards and eat tiny stones to aid digestion.

WHAT EATS CROCODILES?

In Australia, humans are the only animals that hunt and eat adult crocodiles. Crocodile eggs and juveniles are food for birds of prey, snakes, dingoes and goannas. Feral animals, such as dogs and wild pigs may also learn to hunt baby crocodiles. Cane toads are poisonous and will kill crocodiles that eat them.

WHY DO CROCODILES ROLL VIOLENTLY IN THE WATER?

Rolling while holding onto prey allows the crocodile to break meat into smaller pieces that can be swallowed easily.

HOW DO CROCODILES COMMUNICATE?

Adult crocodiles make low, rumbling noises that travel through the water, alerting other crocs to their presence. They also produce smells that have meanings for other crocodiles.

Baby crocodiles make a chirping noise as they are about to hatch. The female hears this and starts to dig the nest open, letting the babies out. She then carries them to the water in her mouth.

A hissing or coughing crocodile is about to attack, so keep away!

A male will slap the water with its head and blow bubbles as ways of warning off other males and attracting females in the area. Males fight and may kill each other in disputes over territories.

As a warning when they feel threatened, some crocodiles shake their bodies to make the water vibrate around them.

WHERE TO SEE CROCODILES

In Australia, most zoos and animal parks have crocodiles on display.

The safest way to see crocodiles in the wild is by joining a crocodile-spotting tourist excursion, run by experienced operators. They will know the best places and times of the day to see crocodiles in the water and out sunning themselves on land.

Trying to find a wild crocodile by standing near the water's edge can be disastrous. You will not see the crocodile until it leaps out of the water and runs towards you.

Crocodiles move quickly to attack from the water

WHAT ABOUT ALLIGATORS?

Alligators have a broader snout than crocodiles and their teeth do not show when they close their mouth.

Q.

Are there wild alligators in Australia?

A.

No. Alligators are not the same as crocodiles, and do not live in the wild in Australia.

American alligator

Tourist boat in Kakadu National Park

Alligator

CROCODILES AND THE ENVIRONMENT

Crocodiles become very aggressive over food

Crocodiles are aggressive in their search for food. They are so strong and large that no other animal can attack them. This makes them an apex predator, which means that they are at the top of their food chain.

Other apex predators in the wild include sharks and lions. These animals are dangerous hunters, but they play very important roles in their ecosystems.

EVOLUTION AND APEX PREDATORS

Apex predators keep an ecosystem healthy by preying on sick and slower animals. This action has a role in evolution, as only the fitter and stronger prey animals live to produce offspring. In time, this leads to a population that is better able to survive in its environment.

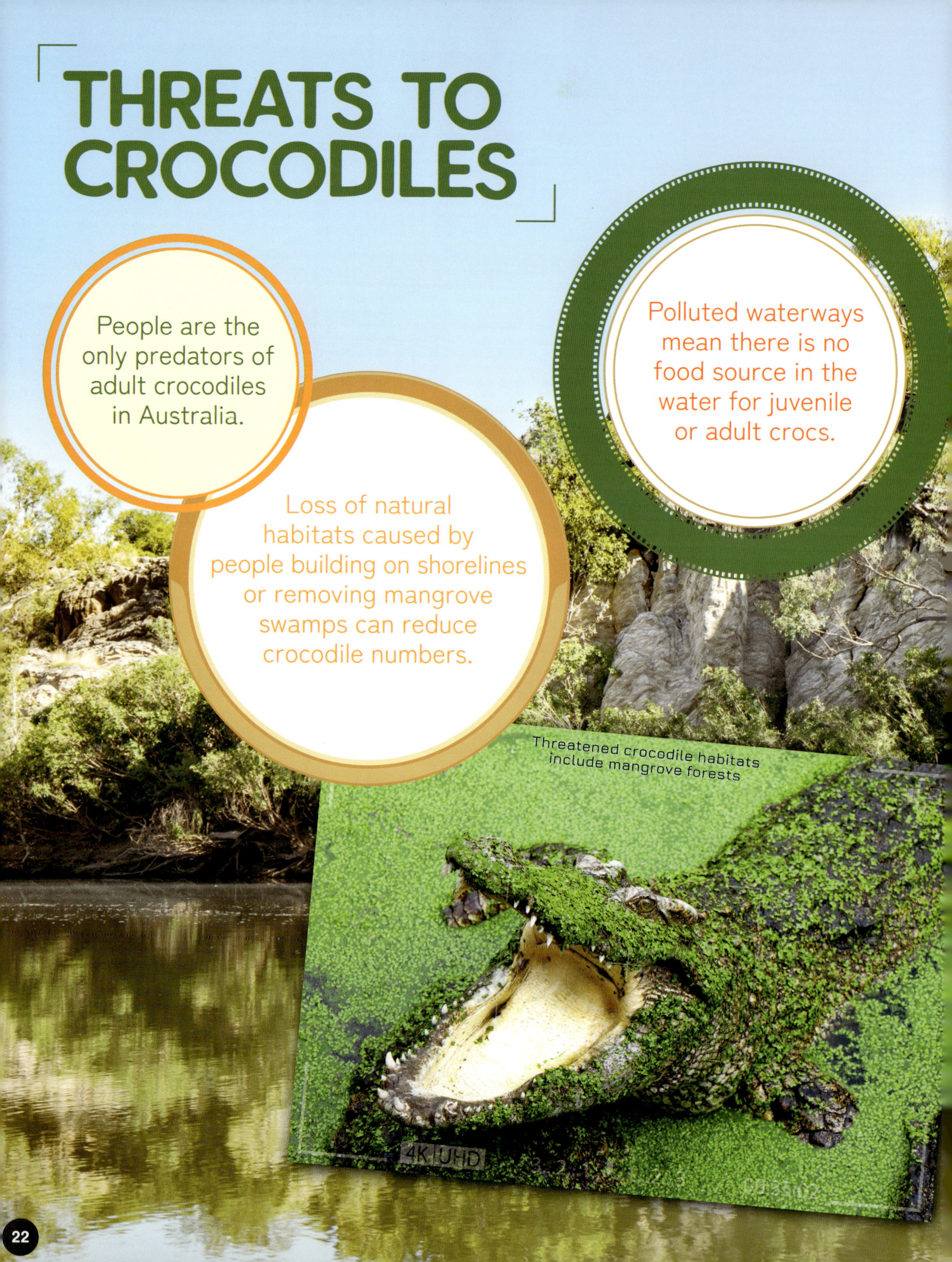

THREATS TO CROCODILES

People are the only predators of adult crocodiles in Australia.

Loss of natural habitats caused by people building on shorelines or removing mangrove swamps can reduce crocodile numbers.

Polluted waterways mean there is no food source in the water for juvenile or adult crocs.

Threatened crocodile habitats include mangrove forests

A large number of baby crocodiles are eaten by other animals.

Floods can destroy crocodile nests. Crocodiles need a safe space to build their nests underground, where they cannot be disturbed. Nests are vulnerable to flooding, habitat destruction by humans and some predators that eat the eggs. Unsuccessful nests lead to declining crocodile numbers.

PEOPLE AND CROCODILES

People are fascinated by the size, danger and unpredictability of the crocodile. This makes the crocodile feeding time at zoos very popular.

CROCODILES DO NOT MAKE GOOD PETS

Since crocodiles are native animals, it is illegal to take eggs or the animal from the wild. Some parts of Australia do allow people to keep pet crocodiles, but only under very strict conditions.

Baby crocodile

SHARING THE BEACHES AND RIVERS

Crocodiles make swimming unsafe in some parts of Australia's north.

CROCODILE MEAT

Crocodile meat is on the menu in many restaurants in Australia. The meat comes from farmed animals, often ones that have been grown from eggs. Some eggs are collected from the wild, while others are laid at the farms. Hunting crocodiles is against the law, except by people with special licences.

SKINS

Licensed hunters or crocodile farmers provide fashion designers with crocodile skins to turn into expensive shoes and bags.

Crocodile leather shoes and belt

RELOCATION

Crocodiles that choose to live in places where there is a high human population are usually relocated to farms or zoos rather than killed.

Crocodiles in the Northern Territory have been able to find their way back to their original home after being relocated to another place in the wild. Sometimes this meant that they travelled over many kilometres.

Crocodile trap

CROCODILES AND INDIGENOUS AUSTRALIANS

Crocodiles are important animals in Australian Indigenous culture. They feature in the Dreaming and in art.

Indigenous Australians have been hunting and coexisting with crocodiles in northern Australia for many thousands of years. Ancient rock art in the area shows crocodiles in the distinctive 'x-ray' art style.

Crocodile rock art in Ubirr, Australia

THE FUTURE OF CROCODILES

While crocodiles are dangerous and do hunt humans, they have been on Earth for 200 million years, making them a species that even survived the extinction of the dinosaurs.

Australian crocodiles numbers are not currently under threat, but human intervention and environmental change mean their future must still be carefully managed.

Crocodiles are part of an intricate ecological system, and a change in any part of that system can affect them. Pollution, changes in the climate, or large-scale destruction of their food sources or habitats could reduce their numbers in the future.

WHAT IS A HERPETOLOGIST?

If you are interested in science and would like to study the biology of crocodiles, you could become a herpetologist (a person who studies reptiles).

SORTING ANIMALS INTO GROUPS

Biologists divide all living things around the world into groups. They call this process classification.

Here are the basic groups that describe all animals with backbones:

AMPHIBIANS

Examples include frogs and salamanders. Amphibians start life in water but later grow lungs so they can breathe air on land.

MAMMALS

Examples include dingoes and possums. Mammals are warm-blooded, have fur and feed their young on milk.

FISH

Examples include sharks and goldfish.

BIRDS

Examples include emus and penguins. Birds are the only animals with feathers.

REPTILES

Examples include lizards and snakes. Reptiles are cold-blooded and are covered in scales.

Mammals are further divided into three main groups:

MONOTREME MAMMALS

Examples include echidnas and platypuses. Monotreme mammals lay eggs.

MARSUPIAL MAMMALS

Examples include kangaroos and koalas. Marsupial mammals produce tiny, underdeveloped babies that continue to grow inside their parent's pouch.

PLACENTAL MAMMALS

Examples include whales and humans. Placental mammals have or once had fur, and they grow their babies inside their bodies.

Humans have a scientific name and a position in the classification of animals. We are called *Homo sapiens*. These Latin words mean 'smart person'.

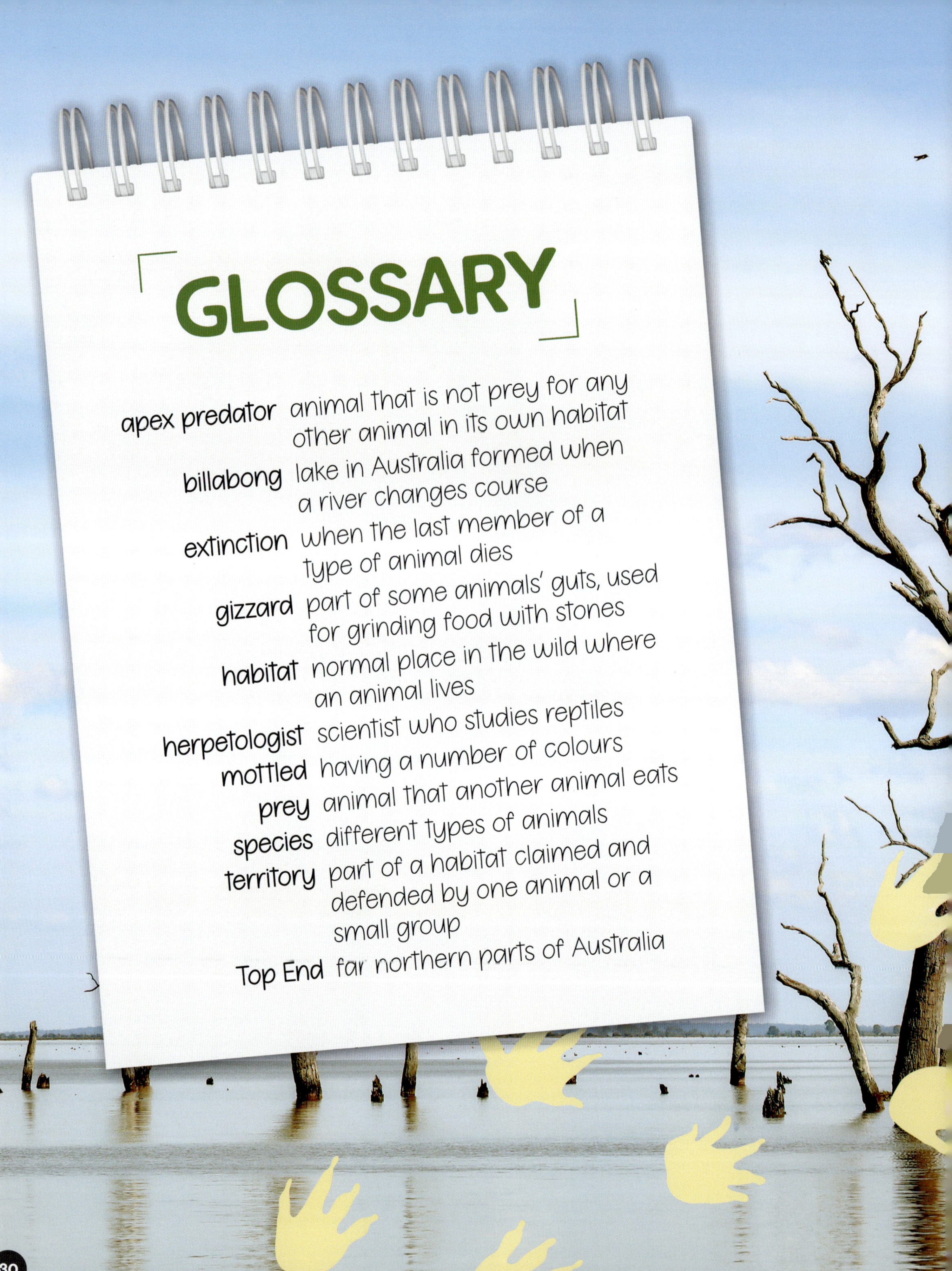

GLOSSARY

apex predator animal that is not prey for any other animal in its own habitat

billabong lake in Australia formed when a river changes course

extinction when the last member of a type of animal dies

gizzard part of some animals' guts, used for grinding food with stones

habitat normal place in the wild where an animal lives

herpetologist scientist who studies reptiles

mottled having a number of colours

prey animal that another animal eats

species different types of animals

territory part of a habitat claimed and defended by one animal or a small group

Top End far northern parts of Australia

Saltwater crocodile in Kakadu National Park
4K UHD
3...2...1...
...1...2...3
00:35:02
00:35:02

INDEX